CENTERING YOURSELF

JOURNAL

WWW.TRUEVINEPUBLISHING.ORG

Centering Yourself
By Dr. Thurman E Webb, Jr.

Published by
True Vine Publishing Co.
810 Dominican Dr.
Nashville, TN 37228
www.TrueVinePublishing.org

Copyright © 2025 by By Dr. Thurman E Webb, Jr.
ISBN: 978-1-968092-00-9
ISBN: 978-1-962783-95-8

All rights reserved. No part of this book may be reproduced in any form or by any electronic or mechanical means, including information storage and retrieval systems, without permission in writing from the publisher, except by a reviewer who may quote brief passages in a review.

Printed in the United States of America—First printing.

TABLE OF CONTENTS

Embracing Self-Responsibility: 11

The Power of self- Reliance: 16

Showing Up in Relationships: 21

Accountability as Empowerment: 26

Embracing Compassionate Service: 31

Sacred Self-Care: 36

The Art of Growth: 41

Quality Over Quantity: 46

Integrity in Action: 51

Being True to Your Word: 56

Building Integrity in Daily Life: 61

Walking the Talk: 65

True Friendship: 70

Cultivating Love in Relationships: 75

The Value of Mutual Support: 80

Nurturing Intimacy: 85

Appreciating Your Friends: 90

Family Ties: 95

The Power of Listening: 100

Dreaming Big: 105

Turning Dreams into Reality: 110

The Importance of Preparation: 115

Creating a Roadmap for Success: 120

Keeping Hope Alive: 125

Setting Goals That Matter: 130

The Power of Self-Awareness: 135

Self-Reflection for Growth: 140

Building Self-Esteem Through Action: 145

Cultivating Self-Confidence: 150

Accepting Yourself Fully: 155

Embracing Change with Grace: 160

Finding Joy in the Present: 165

Cultivating Inner Peace: 170

The Power of Forgiveness: 175

Embracing Patience: 180

Building Mental Resilience: 185

Practicing Kindness: 189

Embracing Vulnerability: 194

Practicing Gratitude for Your Body: 199

Embracing Solitude: 204

Cultivating Creativity: 209

Embracing Simplicity: 214

Practicing Self-Compassion: 219

Building Healthy Boundaries: 224

Cultivating Optimism: 229

Building Self-Discipline: 234

Practicing Mindfulness: 239

Practicing Humility: 244

Fostering Self-Belief: 249

Practicing Acceptance: 254

Cultivating Curiosity: 259

Embracing Joy: 264

Weekly Reflection Log

✓

Reflection Week	WED	FRI
Week 1: Embracing Self-Responsibility	○	○
Week 2: The Power of Self-Reliance	○	○
Week 3: Showing Up in Relationships	○	○
Week 4: Accountability as Empowerment	○	○
Week 5: Embracing Compassionate Service	○	○
Week 6: Sacred Self-Care	○	○
Week 7: The Art of Growth	○	○
Week 8: Quality Over Quantity	○	○
Week 9: Integrity in Action	○	○
Week 10: Being True to Your Word	○	○
Week 11: Building Integrity in Daily Life	○	○
Week 12: Walking the Talk	○	○
Week 13: True Friendship	○	○
Week 14: Cultivating Love in Relationships	○	○

Week 15: The Value of Mutual Support ○ ○
Week 16: Nurturing Intimacy ○ ○
Week 17: Appreciating Your Friends ○ ○
Week 18: Family Ties ○ ○
Week 19: The Power of Listening ○ ○
Week 20: Dreaming Big ○ ○
Week 21: Turning Dreams into Reality ○ ○
Week 22: The Importance of Preparation ○ ○
Week 23: Creating a Roadmap for Success ○ ○
Week 24: Keeping Hope Alive ○ ○
Week 25: Setting Goals That Matter ○ ○
Week 26: The Power of Self-Awareness ○ ○
Week 27: Self-Reflection for Growth ○ ○
Week 28: Building Self-Esteem Through Action ○ ○
Week 29: Cultivating Self-Confidence ○ ○
Week 30: Accepting Yourself Fully ○ ○
Week 31: Embracing Change with Grace ○ ○
Week 32: Finding Joy in the Present ○ ○
Week 33: Cultivating Inner Peace ○ ○
Week 34: The Power of Forgiveness ○ ○

Week 35: Embracing Patience	○	○
Week 36: Building Mental Resilience	○	○
Week 37: Practicing Kindness	○	○
Week 38: Embracing Vulnerability	○	○
Week 39: Practicing Gratitude for Your Body	○	○
Week 40: Embracing Solitude	○	○
Week 41: Cultivating Creativity	○	○
Week 42: Embracing Simplicity	○	○
Week 43: Practicing Self-Compassion	○	○
Week 44: Building Healthy Boundaries	○	○
Week 45: Cultivating Optimism	○	○
Week 46: Building Self-Discipline	○	○
Week 47: Practicing Mindfulness	○	○
Week 48: Practicing Humility	○	○
Week 49: Fostering Self-Belief	○	○
Week 50: Practicing Acceptance	○	○
Week 51: Cultivating Curiosity	○	○
Week 52: Embracing Joy	○	○

> "The path you walk begins the moment you release the weight of excuses—move forward, for you are both the creator and the keeper of your own becoming."

EMBRACING SELF-RESPONSIBILITY:
Owning Your Journey

WEEK 1

Embracing self-responsibility isn't just a shift in thinking—it's an awakening to the idea that we hold the pen in the story of our lives. When we choose to own our journey, we are consciously stepping into the role of both author and artist. We acknowledge that each decision, each step forward, carries us closer to living as our truest selves. Self-responsibility is not about assigning blame or wearing a badge of independence; it's about standing up to say, "I am the one who shapes my experience, and I choose to engage with life fully."

To live with self-responsibility is an act of deep, radical self-love. In doing so, we move away from the notion that life merely "happens" to us. Instead, we step into the awareness that every moment offers a choice. In every interaction and every reaction, we can decide how we want to show up. It's a recognition that even in life's discomforts, we can carve meaning and shape our responses in ways that honor our inner values.

Consider yourself an artist, standing before a vast canvas. The brush is in your hand, the colors and textures are your decisions, and the emerging image is your life. To take responsibility means that you don't wait for someone else to pick up the brush. You lean into the creative process of life, accepting that every stroke—light or dark—brings you closer to a richer, more authentic masterpiece. This act of responsibility brings freedom, the kind that emerges from knowing we are capable of influencing our experience, regardless of what comes our way.

True self-responsibility also calls us to honor boundaries that reflect our well-being. Setting these boundaries isn't about isolation; it's about establishing a foundation where we can stand strong, purposeful, and aligned with our core. When we protect our energy, we cultivate an environment where growth and peace flourish, free from the noise of approval-seeking or distraction. Boundaries allow us to nurture what matters and let go of what does not.

This journey demands courage, but it's a courage fueled by self-respect and an inner commitment to authenticity. The more we practice this, the more our lives reflect a calm and steady alignment with our values. We grow resilient, not because we force control, but because we live in harmony with our own choices and intentions. Embracing self-responsibility means living a life that is, ultimately, in tune with who we are meant to be.

WEEK 01

Wednesday Reflection

Where in your life can you embrace a deeper sense of responsibility this week?

Identify one area—personal, professional, or relational—where you may be waiting for others to act. How can you step into that space with intention and ownership?

_____
_____
_____
_____
_____
_____
_____
_____
_____
_____
_____
_____
_____

WEEK *01*

Friday Reflection

How have you protected your energy and focus this week?

Reflect on any boundaries you set and how they've helped you feel aligned with your values and purpose.

"Even when the way is hidden in mist, trust the power within you to lead—your strength is not in seeing the path, but in stepping boldly, regardless."

THE POWER OF SELF-RELIANCE:
Trusting Yourself to Lead

WEEK 2

Self-reliance is a quiet, powerful strength—a commitment to walking through life with a trust that comes from within. Embracing self-reliance means believing that we already hold the wisdom, tools, and insight necessary to meet the challenges ahead. It's the journey of realizing that while the support of others enriches our lives, our most vital source of strength resides within ourselves. Self-reliance is not a rejection of help but an affirmation of our capacity to lead ourselves, especially when the path seems unclear.

To trust in our own ability to navigate life's complexities is to engage deeply with our own intuition and discernment. Self-reliance is an act of faith in our capacity to rise, not just when things are easy, but in moments when life stretches us. There will always be times when doubt whispers, when the perfect moment seems elusive, or when others may not fully understand our path. Yet, true self-reliance asks us to lead ourselves anyway, embracing each step as a learning moment that builds resilience and self-assuredness.

With self-reliance, we find that courage does not mean living without fear; it means moving forward despite it. This journey of trusting oneself is a layered process that calls for compassion, humility, and a willingness to adapt. Each step we take teaches us more about who we are, and in these small acts of courage, we uncover a well of confidence and inner stability. Self-reliance liberates us from waiting for external validation or the "right" conditions. We start to realize that every decision, even the small ones, is a brick in the foundation of a life built on personal integrity and self-trust.

This resilience becomes our anchor, helping us weather change and uncertainty. By embracing self-reliance, we create a space within ourselves that is both steady and expansive—a place that welcomes growth and transformation. We learn to stand firmly in the belief that we are enough, exactly as we are, capable of moving forward in alignment with our values, goals, and dreams.

WEEK

Wednesday Reflection

How have you taken ownership of your actions this week?

Reflect on a recent situation where you relied on your own judgment, and consider how that strengthened your sense of self-reliance.

WEEK

Friday Reflection

What challenges did you encounter this week that required resilience?

How did trusting yourself help you face these moments? Reflect on how leaning into self-reliance has influenced your journey.

_____
_____
_____
_____
_____
_____
_____
_____
_____
_____
_____
_____
_____
_____
_____

" *In each meeting of hearts lies the chance to offer compassion and truth—arrive with your whole being, and let love speak its language through you.* "

SHOWING UP IN RELATIONSHIPS:
NURTURING CONNECTION AND RESPONSIBILITY

WEEK 3

Taking responsibility in relationships is about making an intentional commitment to show up—fully, honestly, and with a heart open to understanding. Relationships are the spaces where we share our lives and our vulnerabilities, and each connection we have, whether with family, friends, or colleagues, is an opportunity to be present and purposeful. Showing up means engaging from a place of compassion and respect, even when circumstances challenge us.

In our relationships, responsibility calls us to be mindful of the energy we bring. It's asking ourselves: "Am I contributing to an environment of respect, empathy, and mutual support?" This approach isn't about perfection; rather, it's about awareness. By recognizing our impact, we can consciously create spaces that invite warmth and trust. Relationships thrive when both people feel seen and valued, and taking responsibility for our presence in them means actively contributing to that sense of safety.

An essential part of showing up in relationships involves honoring boundaries—both our own and those of others. This balance creates a dynamic of mutual respect, where each person feels free to express their needs and be heard. Responsibility in relationships is about nurturing that balance, understanding that healthy connections are built on a foundation of give and take, where both voices matter.

True responsibility also includes accountability. It means acknowledging when we've fallen short and showing a willingness to repair. Being accountable is not about avoiding mistakes; it's about recognizing them and choosing to make amends, to learn, and to grow. Accountability reinforces the stability of our connections, helping build the kind of trust that can weather challenges.

In relationships, showing up isn't just a gift to others; it's an act of love toward ourselves. It's a choice to engage in a way that uplifts, strengthens, and respects the bond we share. When we bring this level of responsibility to our connections, we cultivate spaces where understanding flourishes, and both people can feel supported in becoming their truest selves.

WEEK

Wednesday Reflection

How have you shown consistency and accountability in your relationships this week?

Reflect on a moment where your presence made a positive impact on someone you care about.

WEEK 03

Friday Reflection

In what ways have you practiced empathy and adaptability in your relationships?

Think about how tuning into others' needs and setting boundaries have influenced the health of your connections.

> "Accountability is the sacred thread that weaves intention into action—hold your word close, for in it, transformation lives."

ACCOUNTABILITY AS EMPOWERMENT:
HONORING YOUR COMMITMENTS TO SELF AND OTHERS

WEEK 4

Accountability is a powerful commitment to living in alignment with our values. It's the act of standing by our word, not just for the promises we make to others but also for those we make to ourselves. When we hold ourselves accountable, we engage with life authentically and with integrity, reflecting our commitment to growth and self-respect. Accountability isn't about perfection; it's about showing up consistently and choosing actions that align with our deepest intentions.

True accountability begins with a willingness to be honest with ourselves. It calls us to look inward with compassion, acknowledging not only our achievements but also areas where we could improve. While it's easy to deflect responsibility, accountability empowers us to take ownership of our actions. This choice to face our own truths helps us build a sense of self-respect and reinforces a life that genuinely reflects our values.

In relationships, accountability builds a foundation of trust. When others see that we honor our word even when it's challenging, they learn that they can rely on us. Accountability in relationships is about showing up consistently, through both calm and turbulent times, modeling the type of honesty and reliability that strengthens bonds. By holding ourselves accountable, we foster mutual respect, deepening our connections with others.

Accountability is also a profound source of empowerment. When we take responsibility for our actions, we move beyond passively waiting for circumstances to change. Instead, we actively shape our reality, knowing that our choices are the bedrock of our lives. Each time we follow through on a commitment, we strengthen our inner resolve, creating a foundation of confidence, purpose, and integrity.

WEEK 04

Wednesday Reflection

How have you held yourself accountable this week?

Reflect on a moment where you took responsibility for an action or decision and how it contributed to your personal growth.

WEEK *04*

Friday Reflection

In what ways have you practiced accountability in your relationships?

Consider a situation where your commitment strengthened trust and reliability with someone important to you.

> "*Service finds its soul when expectation slips away—give with an open heart, and watch the ripples of your kindness shape the world.*"

EMBRACING COMPASSIONATE SERVICE:
HELPING OTHERS WITHOUT EXPECTATION

WEEK 5

Compassionate service is a quiet yet transformative power—a choice to give freely, fueled by an abundance of love and the simple joy of helping others. Embracing compassionate service means stepping into each day with a heart open to making a difference, not for recognition or reward, but because we recognize the shared humanity that binds us all. It's the realization that kindness has no price and that true generosity arises from the desire to uplift others in both small and meaningful ways.

True service doesn't require grand gestures; it's found in the everyday moments when we offer support, a listening ear, or a warm smile. These acts may seem simple, but they carry profound impact. They remind us that service is about being present and available, helping others feel seen and valued. In these moments, we transcend the boundaries of self-interest, discovering the beauty of contributing to a world built on empathy and mutual respect.

Serving others compassionately also teaches us the importance of boundaries. Supporting someone doesn't mean taking over their journey or rushing their growth; it means standing by, offering help when asked, and trusting their timing. This respectful, non-intrusive support honors each individual's path and reinforces the strength in allowing others to grow and heal in their own way.

Compassionate service enriches not only those we serve but also ourselves. When we help without expectation, we find a sense of peace and purpose that arises from simply knowing we've contributed to someone's well-being. Our lives become a testament to kindness, spreading a ripple effect that encourages others to also act with compassion. The joy of giving freely is transformative, leading us to recognize that every action, no matter how small, has the potential to inspire and uplift.

WEEK 05

Wednesday Reflection

How have you contributed to someone's well-being this week, whether in your community, relationships, or everyday interactions?

Reflect on how this act impacted both the people you helped and your own sense of purpose.

_____
_____
_____
_____
_____
_____
_____
_____
_____
_____
_____
_____
_____

WEEK 05

Friday Reflection

In what ways have you set an example of generosity and compassion this week?

Think about how your actions might have inspired others to embrace kindness in their own lives.

> "Self-care is the quiet wisdom of honoring your limits—by nurturing yourself, you open the doors for your light to shine brighter in the world."

SACRED SELF-CARE:
HONORING BOUNDARIES, NURTURING WELL-BEING

WEEK 6

Self-care is a profound act of honoring ourselves—a practice that acknowledges our worth and the importance of nurturing our well-being. When we prioritize self-care, we're not simply taking time for ourselves; we're building a foundation that allows us to bring strength, resilience, and joy into every area of our lives. Far from being selfish or indulgent, self-care is essential. It sustains our capacity for creativity, compassion, and meaningful engagement with the world around us.

Honoring self-care begins with listening to our bodies, minds, and spirits. It's about tuning into our limits and giving ourselves permission to rest. In a world that often celebrates constant productivity, self-care reminds us that restoration is as vital as action. Self-care is not only about physical rest but also encompasses mental, emotional, and spiritual nourishment. Whether through moments of solitude, time spent with loved ones, creative pursuits, or simply being in nature, self-care is our way of replenishing the well within us so that we can continue to show up fully in our lives.

Setting boundaries is a fundamental aspect of self-care. Boundaries are the lines we draw to protect our energy, focus, and peace. They empower us to engage with others and our work from a place of clarity and purpose. Saying "no" is often the most compassionate act we can do for ourselves because it creates room for us to say "yes" to the things that genuinely align with our values. Boundaries honor our capacity to contribute without overextending, helping us avoid burnout and maintain balance.

Self-care is a practice of self-respect. It's a declaration that we deserve a life that is whole and vibrant, a life that reflects our intrinsic value. By caring for ourselves, we create a space where peace and resilience can flourish, allowing us to bring our best selves to the world. When we embrace self-care as a sacred responsibility, we cultivate a life rooted in joy and balance—a life that lets us move with purpose and contribute meaningfully to others.

WEEK 06

Wednesday Reflection

How have you recognized your limits this week and honored your well-being?

Reflect on a moment when you listened to your body or mind and made the choice to rest or recharge.

WEEK 06

Friday Reflection

How have you set boundaries this week to protect your energy and mental health?

Consider how saying "no" or making time for self-care has helped you maintain balance and focus.

"*Growth is not a place to arrive, but a dance of courage and reflection—take each step, and let it guide you toward becoming.*"

THE ART OF GROWTH:
EMBRACING RESPONSIBILITY, RESILIENCE, AND REFLECTION

WEEK 7

Personal growth is a courageous and humble journey—a commitment to evolving into the best version of ourselves. Taking responsibility for this growth means recognizing that we are both the architects and the artists of our own lives. Growth is not something that happens by accident; it is an intentional choice, made daily, to learn, adapt, and move forward. By embracing growth as a responsibility, we acknowledge the impact we can have on ourselves and on those around us.

At its core, personal growth is a choice we renew with every decision, habit, and interaction. It invites us to be mindful of the energy we bring into each moment and the paths we choose to follow. Rather than waiting passively for change, we take an active role in shaping it, setting goals that align with our values and principles. Growth is not linear; it is a winding path marked by both progress and setbacks. Every challenge is an opportunity to deepen our understanding, to refine our character, and to cultivate resilience. Each step forward strengthens our ability to navigate the world with clarity and purpose.

Self-reflection is a cornerstone of personal growth. By regularly pausing to look inward, we can assess where we are and where we want to be. This reflection allows us to celebrate our progress, recognize areas for improvement, and make meaningful adjustments. With a reflective mindset, even the smallest experience becomes a lesson, offering insight and wisdom. Growth requires us to be both students and teachers of our own lives, learning from our journey while setting an example for others.

To take responsibility for our growth is to honor our evolution. It is a commitment to ourselves, marked by patience and compassion. As we navigate the twists and turns of life, we shape a legacy of authenticity and resilience, leaving a positive impact that extends beyond our own journey. When we embrace personal growth with intention, we cultivate a life that reflects our true selves—a life of purpose, strength, and enduring value.

WEEK

Wednesday Reflection

How have you actively pursued opportunities for personal growth this week?

Reflect on a specific action—whether it's setting a goal, learning something new, or seeking feedback—and how it has contributed to your development.

WEEK 07

Friday Reflection

In what ways have you practiced resilience in the face of challenges this week?

Reflect on how a recent setback or obstacle has helped you strengthen your growth mindset.

> "The essence of life is not in how much, but in how deeply—choose meaning over abundance, and let depth become your richest currency."

QUALITY OVER QUANTITY:
FOCUSING ON MEANINGFUL ACTIONS AND INTENTIONAL LIVING

WEEK 8

In a society driven by the pursuit of "more"—more productivity, more achievements, more possessions—choosing quality over quantity is a profound act of intentionality. It is a choice to engage deeply with life, valuing experiences that bring purpose and fulfillment over mere accumulation. Prioritizing quality is about embracing the essence of mindfulness, savoring the richness of each moment instead of rushing to the next. This shift toward quality challenges us to let go of the incessant drive to produce and instead embrace what brings us true meaning.

Focusing on quality means dedicating our time and energy to what truly matters. Rather than filling our schedules with endless tasks, we step back to invest ourselves in activities that enrich our lives. It could be as simple as a quiet evening with loved ones, time spent on a creative pursuit, or moments of solitude that allow us to reconnect with our inner selves. By choosing quality, we create space for authenticity, allowing our lives to reflect our deepest values and desires. This intentionality brings a sense of purpose that cannot be found in mere busyness.

The principle of quality over quantity extends to our relationships as well. It is not the amount of time we spend with someone that defines the strength of our connection, but the presence and depth we bring to those moments. Prioritizing quality means engaging fully—listening, understanding, and appreciating the people around us. In this way, we cultivate relationships that are not only supportive but also deeply meaningful. We build connections that feel real and grounded, connections that nurture both ourselves and those we care about.

Living with a focus on quality over quantity requires us to slow down and embrace what truly fulfills us. It is an approach that values depth over breadth, inviting us to experience each moment fully rather than rushing past it. When we choose quality, we create a legacy of purpose and joy, a life that resonates with intentionality and love. This approach transforms our everyday actions, encouraging us to build a life that is rich in meaning and aligned with who we are at our core.

WEEK 08

Wednesday Reflection

How have you focused on quality over quantity in your tasks or commitments this week?

Reflect on a moment where you prioritized meaningful, intentional work over simply getting things done.

WEEK

Friday Reflection

In your relationships this week, how have you emphasized the quality of your interactions over the quantity of time spent?

Reflect on a time when being fully present deepened a connection.

> "True integrity arises when your actions flow from the river of your values—this is how you build a life that feels true, whole, and unmistakably yours."

INTEGRITY IN ACTION:
LIVING IN ALIGNMENT WITH YOUR VALUES

WEEK 9

Integrity is the art of living in harmony with our values, crafting a life that resonates with honesty and truth, even when no one else is around to witness it. To live with integrity is to make choices that mirror our inner principles, anchoring us to a path that feels real and grounded. Integrity doesn't demand perfection; rather, it calls for a steadfast commitment to truth, kindness, and respect. It's about honoring our own voice, standing by our word, and moving through the world with authenticity.

Living with integrity requires a continual check-in with ourselves, a gentle but intentional assessment of whether our actions are in sync with our beliefs. Integrity invites us to pause and ask, "Is this choice a reflection of who I truly am?" This question cultivates an inner harmony, a peace that grows from knowing we are honoring our most authentic self. In this practice, integrity becomes a foundation of self-trust, allowing us to navigate life with clarity and conviction.

In relationships, integrity is the backbone of trust. When our words align with our actions, others know they can rely on us, creating a safe space where vulnerability and honest communication can flourish. Integrity in relationships is about being true to both ourselves and to others, showing consistency and respect. This approach strengthens connections, allowing bonds to grow deeper and richer. It is through integrity that we create relationships built on a foundation of mutual respect and authenticity.

Integrity is a practice—a daily choice to live with courage and honesty. It's about showing up as our best selves, even when circumstances are challenging. In choosing integrity, we shape a life that feels whole and meaningful, a life that stands as a reflection of our core values. Each choice grounded in integrity leaves a ripple of positive impact, enhancing both our inner world and the world around us.

WEEK 09

Wednesday Reflection

How have your actions this week aligned with your core values?

Reflect on a moment where you faced a choice and chose to act in a way that upheld your integrity, even when it wasn't the easiest path.

WEEK 09

Friday Reflection

In what ways have you held yourself accountable this week?

Reflect on a situation where you took responsibility for a mistake or followed through on a commitment and how it impacted your self-trust or relationships.

> "Promises are the sacred foundations upon which trust is built—honor them, and you will leave behind a legacy of respect and reliability."

BEING TRUE TO YOUR WORD:
HONORING COMMITMENTS TO YOURSELF AND OTHERS

WEEK 10

Being true to our word is one of the most powerful ways we express integrity and build trust. When we honor our commitments, we affirm that our promises are not just words but genuine intentions that carry weight. Each time we follow through, whether in the big moments or the small, daily acts, we strengthen our sense of self-respect and cultivate a reputation of reliability. Keeping our word isn't solely about meeting grand commitments; it's about showing up consistently in the everyday promises we make to ourselves and others.

Honoring our word begins with setting realistic expectations. Before we say "yes," we take a moment to reflect, ensuring that our commitments align with both our values and our capacity. By avoiding overpromising, we protect our energy and sustain balance in our lives. Following through on what we say, no matter how small, builds inner confidence, reinforcing our belief that we are people of action and intention. Each kept promise fortifies our self-trust and deepens our connection to our values.

In our relationships, being true to our word is the foundation of trust. When we keep our promises, we show others that they matter, creating a bond rooted in respect and mutual reliance. Conversely, even small, broken promises can gradually chip away at trust. Being consistent in our commitments reassures those around us of our respect and sincerity. Through these actions, we build a solid foundation that enhances our connections and brings a sense of reliability to our relationships.

Being true to our word is ultimately about alignment. It's about ensuring that our actions mirror our intentions, cultivating a life of authenticity and trustworthiness. When we commit to something, we give it our best effort, recognizing that each promise kept strengthens our own integrity and our relationships with others. This intentional alignment between words and actions not only inspires trust but also enriches our journey with a sense of purpose and reliability.

WEEK 10

Wednesday Reflection

How have you stayed true to your word this week, either to yourself or others?

Reflect on a promise or commitment you kept and how it strengthened your sense of integrity or improved a relationship.

WEEK

Friday Reflection

In what ways did you ensure your promises were realistic and aligned with your values this week?

Reflect on a moment when you set clear boundaries or made a thoughtful commitment, and how it impacted your trust in yourself or your relationships

> "The essence of integrity lives in the quiet acts of honesty—each small choice builds ripples of trust that echo through life's vast waters."

BUILDING INTEGRITY IN DAILY LIFE:
EMBRACING SMALL ACTS WITH BIG IMPACT

WEEK 11

Integrity is not always tested in grand moments. It whispers in the seemingly invisible choices we make when no one is watching—the quiet returns, the honest no's, the follow-through on a promise that felt small when spoken but looms large in the heart of another.

This week, I invite you to pause and ask: *Where am I choosing convenience over alignment? What small act today can be a declaration of who I am becoming?*

We often think of legacy in terms of big achievements, but it's the everyday actions, returning a message, respecting a boundary, offering an unprompted apology, that truly shape our character.

Choose one area of your life, home, work, friendship, or self, and commit to a daily act of integrity. Not perfection. Just presence. Just truth. Just one consistent action that says, *"I see who I am when no one else does—and I still choose to be whole."*

WEEK 11

Wednesday Reflection

Is there a small, quiet act I've done this week that no one noticed, but that I'm deeply proud of?

WEEK 11

Friday Reflection

In what ways did I show up for my values this week, even when it was hard or unnoticed?

> "The clearest reflection of your values lies not in your words, but in your deeds—consistency turns belief into the very fabric of your character."

WALKING THE TALK:
LIVING YOUR VALUES EVERY DAY

WEEK 12

"Walking the talk" is about embodying our values, turning the beliefs we hold dear into actions that define our everyday lives. Speaking of kindness, honesty, or resilience is one thing, but living these values, especially in challenging moments, is where our character truly emerges. Walking the talk is an act of authenticity, a commitment to showing up as the person we aspire to be, not just in easy times, but in moments that demand resilience and integrity.

When we walk our talk, we build a foundation of trust both within ourselves and with those around us. Others recognize that our words are more than just intentions—they're commitments that guide our actions. This consistency doesn't only strengthen our relationships; it also nurtures our self-respect. Each time we choose to live in alignment with our values, we cultivate an inner harmony, a sense of peace that comes from knowing we're honoring our deepest principles.

Living our values isn't about achieving flawlessness; it's about embracing honesty and humility. Walking the talk invites us to reflect on where we can improve, to acknowledge when we fall short, and to recommit to the values we hold. This ongoing dedication to self-awareness and growth is what builds resilience, making us not only more reliable but also more compassionate and forgiving with ourselves and others.

In relationships, walking the talk deepens connection and trust. When others see us living our beliefs consistently, they feel respected, valued, and safe in our presence. This authenticity becomes a form of leadership, inspiring those around us to act with similar integrity. Walking the talk creates a ripple effect, encouraging positive change and fostering deeper, more meaningful connections. Ultimately, it's about crafting a life that reflects our values—a life that is true, whole, and impactful.

WEEK

Wednesday Reflection

How have your actions this week reflected the values you express?

Consider a moment where you "walked the talk," ensuring that your behavior aligned with what you stand for and how that strengthened your integrity.

WEEK 12

Friday Reflection

In what ways have you strengthened trust in your relationships this week by aligning your actions with your words?

Reflect on a situation where your consistency helped deepen mutual respect and connection.

> "A true friend is both a mirror and a refuge—where you catch glimpses of your highest self, and are held in acceptance, without need for explanation."

TRUE FRIENDSHIP:
EMBRACING AUTHENTIC CONNECTIONS AND DEEP SUPPORT

WEEK 13

True friendship is one of life's rare and precious gifts—a bond rooted in love, trust, and an enduring commitment to one another. Unlike relationships built on convenience or circumstance, true friendship is a choice to show up consistently, through life's highs and lows. A true friend sees us fully, without pretense, and accepts us just as we are. They hold space for our dreams, our vulnerabilities, and our joys, becoming a sanctuary where we can be unapologetically ourselves without fear of judgment.

True friendship extends beyond shared memories; it's sustained by honesty, respect, and the courage to have difficult conversations. A genuine friend won't shy away from offering gentle truths, even when the words are hard to hear, because they prioritize our well-being and growth. In times of struggle, they are our steady support, and in moments of victory, they celebrate us wholeheartedly. This bond is sacred, built on mutual understanding and a shared commitment to uplift and nurture each other's spirits.

At the heart of true friendship is reciprocity—a balance of giving and receiving. In these relationships, both people contribute, knowing that support flows both ways. True friends stand by each other not out of obligation but from a place of deep love and shared resilience. This reciprocity creates a foundation of strength, allowing each person to face life's challenges with the knowledge that they are not alone.

True friendship is about being fully present, offering a listening ear, and sharing love that heals and uplifts. It is a partnership of souls, a connection that enriches our lives and reminds us of our inherent worth. By cherishing and nurturing these bonds, we create friendships that sustain us and help us grow in ways we could never achieve alone.

WEEK 13

Wednesday Reflection

How have your friendships provided a space for you to be your authentic self this week?

Reflect on a moment where a friend offered support or understanding that made a difference.

WEEK 13

Friday Reflection

How can you show up with that same level of compassion and honesty in your friendships?

Reflect on how you might deepen a connection by offering support or simply being present.

"Love grows in the soil of empathy—tend to it with care, and your connections will endure, rooted in the deep understanding that only the heart can offer."

CULTIVATING LOVE IN RELATIONSHIPS:
BUILDING CONNECTIONS ROOTED IN EMPATHY AND CARE

WEEK 14

Love is more than a fleeting emotion; it's an ongoing, deliberate practice that we nurture with intention and care. Whether in romance, friendship, or family connections, cultivating love means fostering an environment where empathy, respect, and open communication can thrive. Loving deeply requires seeing the other person in their entirety, understanding their needs, supporting their growth, and accepting them as they are. Love in relationships is about co-creating a space that feels safe, accepting, and uplifting.

At the core of loving relationships is the willingness to listen without judgment. When we listen in this way, we create a sanctuary where each person feels valued and understood. True connection deepens through vulnerability—by sharing our own truths, we invite others to do the same, strengthening the bond with authenticity. Love is enriched when we make space for each other's emotions, celebrate each other's joys, and offer solace during difficult times. This is where love transcends words and becomes an active, lived experience.

Empathy is the cornerstone of love, the bridge that allows us to connect on a deeper level. When we take the time to understand another person's perspective, we honor their unique journey and acknowledge the shared experience of being human. Loving someone means embracing the complexity of their life, recognizing their triumphs and challenges, and standing by them in their struggles and in their joy. Through empathy, we let our loved ones know they are not alone.

Cultivating love requires intentional choices to support, uplift, and create joy together. It's about building a relationship that honors the humanity in both people, with care and respect as its foundation. When we make the conscious choice to invest in love, we create connections that are meaningful, transformative, and lasting. True love, rooted in empathy and care, enriches not only the relationship but the lives of everyone involved.

WEEK 14

Wednesday Reflection

In what ways have you practiced open and honest communication in your relationships this week?

Reflect on a moment where you listened with empathy or created a safe space for connection.

WEEK 14

Friday Reflection

How have you intentionally prioritized love in your relationships this week?

Reflect on a specific moment where you made a conscious effort to nurture a bond and how it impacted both you and the other person.

"In the dance of giving and receiving, balance is the rhythm that sustains—true support lifts both the one who offers and the one who accepts."

THE VALUE OF MUTUAL SUPPORT:
GIVING AND RECEIVING WITH BALANCE

WEEK 15

Mutual support is the lifeblood of relationships that are healthy, balanced, and deeply fulfilling. Whether in friendships, family connections, or romantic partnerships, the dance of giving and receiving creates a space where each person feels valued, empowered, and understood. Mutual support isn't about grand gestures; it's about being there in ways that matter—offering help, encouragement, or simply a listening ear when it's needed most. This kind of support honors each person's well-being without the need to keep score or expect anything in return.

In relationships, support manifests in our presence, whether by assisting with a task, offering comforting words, or providing stability during tough times. Giving support is a natural expression of care, while receiving support requires a willingness to be vulnerable and to trust. Allowing ourselves to receive reminds us that we don't have to bear life's burdens alone, that there is strength in leaning on others who genuinely care.

Mutual support fosters resilience within relationships. Life's highs and lows are inevitable, but knowing there is someone by our side who cares can make the journey less daunting. When we support each other, we create a safe haven, a place where both individuals can find strength, regroup, and recharge. This balanced exchange of support enriches the bond, establishing a foundation where each person can grow and thrive.

At its core, mutual support is about showing up fully, creating a bond rooted in respect, kindness, and trust. It's a reminder that relationships are partnerships in which giving and receiving are reciprocal, an act of shared humanity. When we approach relationships with an open heart, embracing both giving and receiving, we build connections that uplift and inspire us, bringing greater depth and meaning to our lives.

WEEK 15

Wednesday Reflection

How have you shown up to support someone in your life this week?

Reflect on a specific instance where your presence or assistance made a difference for someone.

WEEK

Friday Reflection

How have you allowed yourself to receive support this week?

Consider a moment when you accepted help or encouragement from someone and how it strengthened your connection.

> "*Intimacy blossoms where vulnerability dares to enter—reveal your heart with trust, and watch connection bloom in the space between.*"

NURTURING INTIMACY:
DEEPENING RELATIONSHIPS THROUGH VULNERABILITY AND UNDERSTANDING

WEEK 16

Intimacy is the art of truly knowing and being known—a deep emotional connection that transcends surface-level interactions and brings a sense of closeness and belonging. It's a sacred space where both people feel safe to reveal their true selves, sharing their dreams, fears, and struggles without fear of judgment. Nurturing intimacy requires vulnerability—the courage to be open and to trust that our authentic selves will be accepted. This kind of connection doesn't just enhance relationships; it transforms them into sources of profound support and understanding.

Emotional intimacy is cultivated through meaningful conversations and an unwavering willingness to listen. It's about holding space for each other's emotions with compassion, allowing each person to feel truly seen and valued. Understanding is at the heart of intimacy; even when we don't fully agree, we make the effort to empathize and appreciate the other person's perspective. This bridge of connection brings us closer, fostering a sense of compassion and attunement that strengthens the bond.

Quality time is essential to nurturing intimacy. By spending undistracted time together—whether through quiet conversation, shared activities, or simply being in each other's presence—we deepen our connection. These moments create memories and become the foundation of a lasting relationship. Physical intimacy may also play a role in some connections, but the heart of true intimacy lies in emotional closeness and trust.

Nurturing intimacy means creating a sanctuary within the relationship, a place where both people feel valued, safe, and loved. By investing in this closeness, we cultivate relationships that are not only meaningful but also healing and transformative. True intimacy brings out the best in us, enriching our lives with connection, empathy, and a shared journey of growth.

WEEK 16

Wednesday Reflection

How have you deepened intimacy in your relationships this week?

Reflect on a moment where you allowed yourself to be vulnerable or truly listened to someone, creating a deeper connection.

WEEK 16

Friday Reflection

What steps have you taken to understand and empathize with someone important to you this week?

Reflect on how this act of empathy or quality time has nurtured intimacy in your relationship.

> "Gratitude deepens the roots of friendship—celebrate those who walk beside you, not just in joy but through every challenge life brings."

APPRECIATING YOUR FRIENDS:
CULTIVATING GRATITUDE IN FRIENDSHIP

WEEK 17

Friendship is one of life's most profound gifts—a connection rooted in trust, shared experiences, and unwavering support. Yet, amid the demands of everyday life, we may sometimes overlook the importance of expressing our gratitude for those who stand by us, bringing comfort, laughter, and encouragement. Cultivating gratitude in our friendships means pausing to recognize and celebrate the unique qualities each friend brings to our lives. It's about honoring the laughter, the quiet moments, the late-night talks, and the memories that make these relationships so cherished.

When we take time to appreciate our friends, we deepen the bond we share. Small gestures of gratitude—a sincere "thank you," a thoughtful note, or a kind act—can have lasting effects on both people. These expressions of appreciation reinforce the importance of the friendship and remind both of you of the value you bring into each other's lives. Gratitude becomes a source of strength and joy, creating a positive flow that uplifts and nourishes the connection.

Appreciating our friends also keeps us grounded in the present, reminding us of the beauty and blessing of having companions who journey with us. Friendships, like all relationships, require care, presence, and acknowledgment. By celebrating our friends and letting them know how much they mean to us, we create a resilient foundation for the relationship, allowing it to thrive over time.

Expressing gratitude in friendship is a choice—to be present, to notice the small things, and to let our friends know they are cherished. It's a daily reminder that friendship is a gift we choose to nurture, and that each act of gratitude strengthens the connection, deepening the love and respect shared.

WEEK

Wednesday Reflection

How have you expressed gratitude for your friends this week?

Reflect on a moment where you showed appreciation and how it deepened your bond.

WEEK

Friday Reflection

How have your friends supported or uplifted you recently?

Take a moment to reflect on the blessings of friendship and consider a way to show your gratitude.

> "Family is not merely where you are bound by blood; it is the sacred space where your love, patience, and presence shape the very essence of what comes after you."

FAMILY TIES:
UNDERSTANDING YOUR ROLE WITHIN YOUR FAMILY

WEEK 18

Family relationships are some of the most enduring and influential bonds we experience, shaping our understanding of love, support, and connection. To understand our role within the family is to recognize how our actions, words, and presence impact those closest to us. It's about showing up with love, compassion, and respect, acknowledging that each member's contribution is vital to the well-being of the whole. Whether we are parents, siblings, children, or extended family members, each of us holds a unique place and purpose within this interconnected web.

Our roles within the family naturally evolve over time, often shifting as we mature and navigate life's many changes. By understanding our place within the family structure, we can respond with empathy and intention, offering support that aligns with both our values and the needs of those around us. This support might mean lending guidance, providing a listening ear, or simply being present through both joy and adversity. By honoring our role, we help to foster an environment grounded in mutual respect and unconditional love.

Family can bring both profound joy and complex challenges. Close-knit bonds can lead to misunderstandings, but when we recognize our role, we are better equipped to approach family dynamics with patience and understanding. By bringing compassion into our family relationships, we contribute to a legacy of kindness and resilience, setting an example that can inspire and guide future generations.

Our role within the family is one of presence, connection, and unwavering support. Showing up with love and a willingness to grow together strengthens both our family bonds and our own sense of belonging. By embracing this role, we cultivate a family foundation rooted in love and resilience, one that we can carry forward with pride and gratitude.

WEEK

Wednesday Reflection

How have you shown up for your family this week?

Reflect on a moment where your actions or words positively impacted a family member.

WEEK *18*

Friday Reflection

How has understanding your role within your family influenced your relationships this week?

Reflect on a time when you responded with empathy, contributing to a more loving and supportive family environment.

> "True listening is a gift of presence—when you hear with your heart, the silence between words becomes the birthplace of connection."

THE POWER OF LISTENING:
DEEPENING CONNECTIONS THROUGH TRUE PRESENCE

WEEK 19

Listening is one of the most profound ways to connect with others. In a world that often celebrates speaking over listening, the act of truly hearing someone becomes a gift of care, respect, and empathy. To listen fully, without interruption or judgment, is to create a safe space where the other person feels seen, valued, and understood. Listening goes beyond just hearing words; it involves tuning into the emotions, intentions, and needs behind those words, allowing us to connect on a deeper level.

True listening demands presence and patience. It means setting aside our own thoughts, reactions, and judgments, and focusing entirely on the person before us. This level of attentiveness shows that we're not merely hearing, but genuinely striving to understand. When people feel truly heard, they're more likely to open up and share their authentic selves, strengthening the trust and depth within the relationship.

Listening also builds empathy by inviting us to step into another person's world, experiencing their perspectives and emotions. It reminds us of our shared humanity and fosters a deep understanding. In times of conflict, listening can bridge divides, minimize misunderstandings, and open the door to resolution. By fully engaging in the act of listening, we create opportunities for connection, compassion, and healing, building bridges even in the most challenging conversations.

Listening is ultimately an act of love and humility. It's an acknowledgment that each person has a unique story and perspective, and that by listening, we honor their dignity and worth. This simple yet powerful practice strengthens our relationships, enriches our lives, and brings us closer to the people who matter most.

WEEK *19*

Wednesday Reflection

How have you practiced active listening this week?

Reflect on a moment where you focused on understanding someone fully, and how it impacted your connection.

WEEK 19

Friday Reflection

In what ways has listening deeply influenced your relationships this week?

Consider a conversation where your presence helped someone feel valued or understood.

> "Dream with wild courage, for in every vision lives the power to reshape your world—and to inspire those who are touched by your light."

DREAMING BIG:
EMBRACING THE POWER OF VISION AND POSSIBILITY

WEEK 20

Dreaming big is the courageous act of envisioning a future filled with limitless potential and purpose. It's about allowing ourselves to imagine the life we truly desire, unrestrained by self-doubt or the limitations imposed by fear. Dreams are the seeds of our aspirations, lighting a path toward growth and inspiring us to take bold steps toward what matters most. When we dare to dream big, we create a vision that invigorates us, giving our lives direction and meaning.

Dreaming on a grand scale doesn't mean ignoring reality; instead, it's the art of looking beyond present circumstances, trusting in our ability to grow, adapt, and achieve. Big dreams often require us to step out of our comfort zones, asking us to embrace new challenges and uncertainty. This journey demands courage, but it's also deeply fulfilling, as we discover new facets of ourselves and uncover strengths we didn't know we had. Each step toward our dreams is a reflection of our resilience and our faith in possibility.

Dreams also provide a framework for setting meaningful goals, breaking down our vision into actionable, achievable steps. By focusing on these small steps, we make steady progress, transforming along the way. Dreaming big isn't about racing to the finish line; it's about savoring the journey, growing from each experience, and honoring every moment that brings us closer to who we are meant to be.

At its core, dreaming big is about believing in our potential and embracing the extraordinary. It's about living a life that aligns with our passions and values, a life that feels rich, inspired, and purposeful. When we hold on to our dreams, we not only craft a future that excites us but also inspire others to envision and pursue their own possibilities.

WEEK

Wednesday Reflection

What dreams have you been nurturing this week?

Reflect on a vision or aspiration that brings you joy and consider what small steps you can take to move closer to it.

WEEK 20

Friday Reflection

How has dreaming big influenced your actions or decisions this week?

Reflect on a moment where your vision inspired you to step out of your comfort zone or approach a situation with a renewed sense of possibility.

> "Dreams are only bridges to reality when stepped upon—lay each stone with intention, and watch the world of possibilities take form beneath your feet."

TURNING DREAMS INTO REALITY:
TAKING PRACTICAL STEPS TOWARD YOUR GOALS

WEEK 21

Dreams inspire us, serving as guiding lights toward what we want most, but transforming dreams into reality requires dedication, planning, and steady action. This journey is about harnessing the energy of our dreams and channeling it into tangible, practical steps—creating a bridge between where we are and where we aim to be. By setting specific goals and embracing the process, we build a clear path that transforms dreams into achievable milestones.

The first step in bringing dreams to life is breaking them down into manageable goals. Large visions can feel overwhelming, but by focusing on small, intentional actions, we create a sense of momentum. Each completed goal becomes a stepping stone toward our vision, building confidence with every achievement. Crafting a plan that includes realistic timelines, available resources, and supportive networks helps keep us grounded and motivated, even through inevitable challenges.

Consistency is the cornerstone of progress. Real transformation often results from the cumulative effect of small steps taken daily. It's not about reaching the destination overnight; it's about honoring the journey, celebrating each milestone, and learning from setbacks. Challenges along the way don't signal the end of our dreams but invite us to adapt, strengthen our resolve, and refine our path.

Turning dreams into reality requires persistence, resilience, and a commitment to keep moving, even when the way forward isn't entirely clear. Each step we take aligns us more closely with our vision, inching us toward a life filled with purpose and fulfillment. In the end, our dreams become the foundation of a life that reflects our dedication, courage, and growth.

WEEK 21

Wednesday Reflection

What small steps have you taken this week toward achieving your dreams?

Reflect on one action you took to move closer to your goals, and how it brought you a sense of progress.

WEEK 21

Friday Reflection

How have you adapted to challenges on your path toward your dreams this week?

Consider a moment where you encountered an obstacle and reflect on how resilience has helped you continue moving forward.

> "Preparation is quiet faith in your future—the work you lay down today is the foundation of tomorrow's unfolding success."

THE IMPORTANCE OF PREPARATION:
BEING READY FOR OPPORTUNITIES

WEEK 22

Preparation is the bedrock of success, a vital practice that enables us to embrace opportunities when they arise. As the saying goes, "luck is when preparation meets opportunity," and it holds great wisdom. By preparing ourselves—through learning, refining our skills, and developing supportive habits—we increase our readiness to seize moments of growth and advancement. Preparation transforms potential into reality, turning our goals into attainable steps forward.

Effective preparation begins with clarity. Knowing what we want and setting intentions aligned with our values provides the direction we need. This clarity helps us focus our energy, channeling it into actions that support our vision. Preparation also requires patience and persistence as we work diligently behind the scenes, trusting that our efforts will bring positive results. Each moment invested in preparation becomes a stepping stone toward future opportunities.

Preparation builds confidence, too. When we take the time to hone our skills, expand our knowledge, or establish strong routines, we feel more capable of handling new challenges. This readiness empowers us to approach opportunities with courage and decisiveness. Whether the opportunity is a career move, a new relationship, or a personal goal, preparation gives us the foundation we need to say "yes" with confidence and clarity.

Preparation allows us to live proactively rather than reactively. By staying prepared, we open ourselves to a world of possibilities, knowing we've laid the groundwork to make the most of them. When we prepare with purpose and intention, we align ourselves with opportunities that move us closer to our dreams, enhancing both our readiness and our resilience.

WEEK 22

Wednesday Reflection

What steps have you taken to prepare for your goals or future opportunities this week?

Reflect on a specific action that has helped you feel more ready and confident.

WEEK 22

Friday Reflection

How has your preparation influenced your actions or mindset this week?

Consider a moment where feeling prepared empowered you to make a decision or seize an opportunity.

> "A clear plan is the canvas upon which your dreams take shape—paint it with intention, and let your vision lead you toward the masterpiece of your life."

CREATING A ROADMAP FOR SUCCESS:
PLANNING WITH PURPOSE AND VISION

WEEK 23

Success is more than reaching a destination; it's about crafting a journey of intentional planning and purposeful action. A roadmap for success serves as our guiding blueprint, aligning our daily actions with our long-term goals and core values. By creating a clear, actionable plan, we turn our dreams into achievable steps, empowering ourselves to move forward with confidence and clarity.

Creating an effective roadmap begins by defining what success means to us personally. This vision is unique, shaped by our values, passions, and deepest aspirations. Once we have a clear picture of what we're aiming for, we can break down our goals into smaller, attainable milestones. Each milestone becomes a marker of progress, helping us stay motivated and grounded on our journey. This structured approach prevents overwhelm, offering manageable steps that keep us focused and aligned.

A true roadmap is also adaptable, providing flexibility as life unfolds. While having a plan is essential, it's equally important to remain open to adjustments, understanding that growth and new opportunities may shift our direction. This adaptability keeps us grounded, allowing us to pivot when needed without losing sight of our vision.

Creating a roadmap for success means taking ownership of our future and living with intentionality. It's about making choices that reflect our highest aspirations and building a life that feels true to who we are. With each step we take, we move closer to a life that reflects our purpose and brings us fulfillment.

WEEK 23

Wednesday Reflection

How have you planned purposefully for your goals this week?

Reflect on one action you took that aligned with your long-term vision and helped you feel more connected to your path.

WEEK 23

Friday Reflection

How has flexibility in your roadmap helped you stay adaptable this week?

Consider a moment where you adjusted your plan to better align with changing circumstances or new insights.

> "Hope is the still strength that whispers through darkness—its voice soft, but unwavering, assuring you that light is on the horizon."

KEEPING HOPE ALIVE:
CULTIVATING RESILIENCE THROUGH OPTIMISM

WEEK 24

Hope is the guiding light that keeps us moving forward, especially during life's most challenging times. It's the belief that, regardless of present struggles, a brighter future is possible. Keeping hope alive is a profound act of resilience—it's the decision to see possibilities even when obstacles arise, and to believe in our capacity to create positive change. Hope energizes our dreams, giving us the strength to keep moving forward, even when the path is unclear.

Cultivating hope begins with a mindset of optimism. This doesn't mean ignoring difficulties but rather choosing to focus on growth and learning within each experience. Hope encourages us to seek solutions rather than dwelling solely on problems, fostering a sense of empowerment and resilience. When we hold onto hope, we reinforce our inner strength, recognizing that every setback is a stepping stone toward growth.

Hope is also nurtured through connection. During tough times, reaching out to friends, mentors, or loved ones can help reignite our sense of optimism. Sharing our dreams and concerns with others reminds us that we're not alone and that support is always available. Hope flourishes when we surround ourselves with people who believe in us and in the possibilities of a brighter future.

Keeping hope alive is a daily choice—a practice of believing in the potential for change both within ourselves and in the world around us. With hope, we confront life's uncertainties with courage, knowing that brighter days are on the horizon.

WEEK 24

Wednesday Reflection

How have you maintained hope and optimism this week?

Reflect on a moment where you chose to focus on possibility instead of dwelling on limitations.

WEEK 24

Friday Reflection

How has hope influenced your resilience this week?

Consider a challenge you faced and how hope helped you navigate it with strength and positivity.

"When your goals align with the essence of your values, each step forward carries you closer to the fulfillment that resonates in your soul."

SETTING GOALS THAT MATTER:
ALIGNING AMBITIONS WITH VALUES

WEEK 25

Setting goals is a transformative way to bring purpose and direction into our lives, but the most meaningful goals are those that resonate with our deepest values. Goals that truly matter are not just markers of external success—they reflect what we hold most dear, helping us build a life that feels authentic and fulfilling. When our ambitions align with our core values, each step we take becomes a pathway toward greater personal growth and lasting fulfillment.

The journey of setting meaningful goals begins with self-reflection. By examining what we genuinely value—whether it's health, creativity, relationships, or personal development—we can design goals that enrich these areas. These goals are an expression of who we are and what we believe in, grounding us with a sense of purpose that keeps us committed, even when we encounter challenges.

Aligned goals provide clarity and focus, helping us navigate life with intention. When we understand our "why," we are less susceptible to distractions from short-term gratification or external pressures. Instead, we make choices that bring us closer to the life we envision, fostering a sense of peace and satisfaction. Knowing that our actions reflect our values gives us confidence that we are building something meaningful and enduring.

Setting goals that matter is about crafting a life that resonates with our inner truths and aspirations. It's an ongoing commitment to honor who we are, using our ambitions as tools to create a life of purpose, joy, and fulfillment.

WEEK 25

Wednesday Reflection

What values have guided your goals this week?

Reflect on a specific goal that feels aligned with your core beliefs and how it has inspired your actions.

WEEK 25

Friday Reflection

How has aligning your goals with your values influenced your choices this week?

Consider a moment where your values guided you to make a meaningful decision.

> "To know yourself deeply is to hold the key to intentional living—self-awareness unlocks growth."

THE POWER OF SELF-AWARENESS:
KNOWING YOURSELF DEEPLY

WEEK 26

Self-awareness is the foundation of personal growth and the key to building meaningful relationships. It involves looking inward, exploring our thoughts, emotions, and motivations, and understanding how they influence our actions and interactions. By cultivating self-awareness, we gain a deeper insight into our strengths, our challenges, and the patterns that shape our lives, allowing us to make intentional choices that resonate with who we truly are.

Knowing ourselves deeply requires taking time for reflection, acknowledging both our light and our shadow. It's about being honest with ourselves, understanding our triggers, and questioning the beliefs that influence our worldview. This self-knowledge equips us to face life's challenges with resilience and compassion, transforming habitual reactions into conscious responses that align with our values.

Self-awareness is also transformative in our relationships. When we understand our own emotions and needs, we can communicate more openly and effectively, fostering connection and reducing misunderstandings. By knowing ourselves, we become more empathetic, making space for the experiences and emotions of others, which encourages mutual growth and understanding.

Self-awareness is an ongoing journey—a commitment to lifelong self-discovery and growth. As we deepen our self-understanding, we create a life that feels authentic, purposeful, and in harmony with our core values. This practice of self-awareness serves as a guide, helping us make choices that honor our true selves and lead to a richer, more fulfilling life.

WEEK 26

Wednesday Reflection

How have you practiced self-awareness this week?

Reflect on a moment where you tuned into your emotions or thoughts, and how this insight influenced your actions.

WEEK 26

Friday Reflection

In what ways has self-awareness enhanced your relationships this week?

Consider a time where understanding your own feelings helped you connect more deeply with someone else.

"Through reflection, you turn experience into wisdom—pause, look inward, and let growth begin."

SELF-REFLECTION FOR GROWTH:
THE POWER OF INTROSPECTION

WEEK 27

Self-reflection is a powerful practice that invites us into a journey of personal growth and transformation. By taking time to look inward and examine our thoughts, behaviors, and experiences, we gain insights that deepen our understanding of ourselves. This process helps us celebrate our strengths, recognize our challenges, and identify areas for improvement, guiding us toward intentional growth and positive change.

Introspection is not merely about pinpointing our shortcomings; it's also about honoring our journey and recognizing our achievements. Through reflection, we learn from every experience, embracing both the light and shadow aspects of who we are. Self-reflection provides clarity about what truly matters to us, allowing us to align our actions with our core values and aspirations, and moving us closer to an authentic life.

True growth through reflection requires self-compassion. It's easy to be overly critical, but introspection invites us to approach ourselves with kindness and understanding. When we reflect with compassion, we create a safe space for learning, healing, and growth. This gentle approach fosters resilience and self-acceptance, allowing us to move forward with greater confidence and empowerment.

Self-reflection is a lifelong practice, a tool that nurtures our growth and well-being. By embracing introspection, we unlock our potential and create a path to live authentically and purposefully.

WEEK 27

Wednesday Reflection

How have you practiced self-reflection this week?

Reflect on a specific moment where you looked inward and what insights it revealed about your path or values.

WEEK 27

Friday Reflection

In what ways has self-reflection influenced your growth this week?

Consider a moment where reflecting on a situation helped you make a more conscious, empowered choice.

> "Every step forward affirms your worth—celebrate progress, no matter how small, and watch your confidence grow."

BUILDING SELF-ESTEEM THROUGH ACTION:
CELEBRATING PROGRESS AND ACHIEVEMENTS

WEEK 28

Self-esteem is built not just through positive thoughts but through the actions we take and the progress we make along the way. Each goal we achieve, no matter how small, strengthens our sense of worth, reinforcing our confidence in our abilities. When we set intentions and follow through, we experience a sense of accomplishment that fuels our growth and builds self-belief.

Taking action toward our goals is a powerful way of affirming our value and potential. Every step forward, every effort made, reminds us that we are capable and deserving of success. It's not about immediately reaching the final destination but about recognizing and celebrating each milestone on our journey. These moments of achievement highlight our resilience and strength, reminding us that we have the capacity to grow and thrive.

Building self-esteem through action also requires us to embrace challenges. Often, it's in stepping beyond our comfort zones that we discover our true strengths. By taking risks and confronting our fears, we cultivate a deeper sense of self-worth. Every time we overcome an obstacle, we reinforce our belief in ourselves, creating a foundation of confidence and courage that supports us in future endeavors.

Self-esteem is nurtured through a continuous cycle of action, reflection, and celebration. By honoring our progress, we strengthen our relationship with ourselves, learning to trust in our abilities and embrace our unique potential. Each achievement, no matter how small, adds to a life rich with purpose, fulfillment, and self-assurance.

WEEK 28

Wednesday Reflection

What actions have you taken this week that reflect your commitment to growth?

Reflect on a small achievement that boosted your confidence or sense of self-worth.

WEEK 28

Friday Reflection

How has celebrating your progress influenced your self-esteem this week?

Consider a moment where you acknowledged your efforts, and how it helped you feel more empowered.

> "Self-confidence is built one small success at a time—believe in your steps, and the path will reveal itself."

CULTIVATING SELF-CONFIDENCE:
EMBRACING SMALL SUCCESSES AS STEPPING STONES

WEEK 29

Self-confidence is a quality we build gradually, by recognizing our growth and celebrating our achievements, no matter how small. It's the assurance that we are capable, resilient, and ready to face life's challenges. Building self-confidence doesn't demand grand milestones; it's about embracing the small successes along the way. Every accomplishment, however minor it may seem, strengthens our belief in ourselves and our abilities.

When we take time to celebrate small successes, we create a positive cycle of growth and motivation. Instead of focusing solely on how far we still have to go, we pause to honor the steps we've already taken. Each small victory serves as a reminder that we're making meaningful progress and that every effort counts. This acknowledgment of our journey empowers us to approach future challenges with a sense of courage and optimism.

Embracing small successes also encourages a shift in perspective. Rather than measuring ourselves against others, we focus on our unique path, appreciating each milestone as a testament to our personal growth. This mindset nurtures a deep sense of self-worth and drives us to keep pursuing our goals, knowing that each success is a valuable stepping stone on our journey.

Self-confidence grows from within—it's the result of choosing to show up, to try, and to believe in ourselves consistently. By celebrating small wins, we create a foundation of confidence that supports us across all areas of life, encouraging us to keep moving forward with strength and determination.

WEEK 29

Wednesday Reflection

How have you celebrated small successes this week?

Reflect on a recent achievement, no matter how minor, and how it contributed to your self-confidence.

WEEK 29

Friday Reflection

In what ways has acknowledging your progress influenced your motivation this week?

Consider a moment where you embraced a small success, and how it inspired you to keep moving forward.

"To accept yourself is to embrace your entirety—strengths, flaws, and the beauty of your becoming."

ACCEPTING YOURSELF FULLY:
EMBRACING STRENGTHS AND GROWTH AREAS

WEEK 30

Self-acceptance is a profound act of self-love that involves embracing every part of ourselves—our strengths, our challenges, and all that lies between. It's the recognition that we are whole and worthy, even as we continue to learn and grow. Accepting ourselves fully enables us to move through life with peace and confidence, knowing we don't need to be perfect to be valuable. Instead, we honor our unique journey, celebrating our strengths while also welcoming opportunities for growth.

Embracing our strengths is an essential part of self-acceptance. When we recognize and appreciate our unique qualities and skills, we empower ourselves to share these gifts with the world. Self-acceptance also means embracing our imperfections with compassion. Rather than seeing limitations as flaws, we view them as areas for exploration, learning, and improvement. This gentle approach fosters resilience and helps us grow without harsh self-criticism.

Self-acceptance frees us from the need for constant external validation. When we accept ourselves, we become comfortable in our own skin, trusting that our worth is not defined by others' opinions or societal expectations. This inner confidence allows us to live authentically, crafting a life that feels true to who we are, rather than one shaped by comparison or conformity.

Self-acceptance is an ongoing journey of being gentle with ourselves, appreciating who we are today, and creating space for who we are becoming. By embracing our full selves, we build a foundation of love, respect, and joy that nourishes both our present and our future.

# WEEK 30

Wednesday Reflection

How have you embraced your strengths and unique qualities this week?

Reflect on a moment where you honored what makes you "you" and how it influenced your self-acceptance.

WEEK 30

Friday Reflection

In what ways have you shown compassion toward your growth areas this week?

Consider a time where you accepted an imperfection and viewed it as an opportunity for learning.

"Change invites growth; lean into it with curiosity, and life will unfold in unexpected wonder."

EMBRACING CHANGE WITH GRACE:
NAVIGATING LIFE'S TRANSITIONS

WEEK 31

Change is a constant in life, and learning to embrace it with grace allows us to navigate life's transitions with resilience and inner strength. Whether it's starting a new job, moving to a different place, or experiencing a shift in our personal lives, change invites us to grow, adapt, and expand our perspectives. Embracing change doesn't mean ignoring our discomfort or fears; it means leaning into each experience with curiosity and an open heart, trusting that every transition holds valuable lessons.

When we accept change, we step into a place of empowerment. Instead of resisting or fearing the unknown, we recognize that true growth often comes from stepping beyond our comfort zones. Change can be challenging, yet it offers fresh opportunities for learning, self-discovery, and renewal. By approaching life's transitions with a mindset of possibility, we transform them into steppingstones for our personal and spiritual evolution.

Embracing change also teaches us the power of adaptability. Life rarely unfolds according to our plans, but by learning to flow with its twists and turns, we cultivate a sense of peace and acceptance. This adaptability doesn't require us to be perfect; it simply calls us to face change with courage and a trust in our ability to handle whatever may come. Through this process, we build resilience, a quality that supports us through both expected and unexpected transitions.

Embracing change with grace means finding hope in the unknown and trusting that each chapter of life draws us closer to our truest selves. It's about creating a life that welcomes growth and transformation, a life that reflects our strength, adaptability, and willingness to evolve.

WEEK *31*

Wednesday Reflection

How have you embraced a recent change in your life this week?

Reflect on a moment where you faced a transition with openness and curiosity, and how it has helped you grow.

WEEK 31

Friday Reflection

In what ways has adapting to change influenced your perspective or resilience this week?

Consider a situation where you embraced flexibility and found strength in the process.

> "Joy is not in perfection but in presence—notice the now, and life becomes extraordinary."

FINDING JOY IN THE PRESENT:
CULTIVATING MINDFULNESS AND GRATITUDE

WEEK 32

True joy isn't waiting for life to be perfect; it's embracing each moment with openness and gratitude. Finding joy in the present means cultivating mindfulness, appreciating the beauty of now, and choosing to focus on gratitude for all that we have. By being fully present, we release ourselves from the burdens of past regrets and future anxieties, allowing us to experience life in its fullness, just as it is.

Mindfulness invites us to slow down, to savor each breath, each sensation, and each connection we make. It's the practice of noticing the little things—the warmth of the sun on our skin, the sound of laughter, the peacefulness of a quiet morning. By grounding ourselves in these small, beautiful moments, we connect more deeply with ourselves and the world, discovering joy in the simple act of being alive.

Gratitude complements mindfulness as its powerful partner. When we focus on what we're thankful for, we shift our attention from what might be missing to what is already abundant in our lives. Practicing gratitude reveals that joy isn't something we need to chase; it's already present, woven into the fabric of our everyday experiences. Each expression of gratitude is a reminder of life's blessings, fostering peace, contentment, and a deeper appreciation for the present.

Finding joy in the present is about choosing to live with a heart open to wonder, acceptance, and gratitude. By embracing the moment, we build a life filled with meaning, beauty, and joy, independent of external circumstances. This way of living transforms each day into an opportunity for happiness and fulfillment.

WEEK 32

Wednesday Reflection

How have you found joy in the present moment this week?

Reflect on a small, mindful experience that brought you a sense of peace or happiness.

WEEK 32

Friday Reflection

In what ways has gratitude shaped your perspective this week?

Consider a moment where focusing on what you're thankful for helped you find joy and contentment.

> "Inner peace is a choice; protect your calm, and let it anchor you amidst life's storms."

CULTIVATING INNER PEACE:
FINDING CALM AMIDST LIFE'S BUSYNESS

WEEK 33

Inner peace isn't about escaping life's inevitable challenges; it's about developing a calm center within that allows us to navigate stress and noise with resilience and grace. Cultivating inner peace means making a commitment to nurture serenity, even in chaotic times. This practice invites us to slow down, reconnect with ourselves, and seek moments of stillness that refresh and ground us. By regularly engaging in activities that calm the mind—such as meditation, mindful breathing, journaling, or spending time in nature—we build a resilience that strengthens our ability to handle stress gracefully.

A key to cultivating inner peace is becoming aware of what disrupts our calm and what restores it. Setting boundaries with our time, energy, and attention is essential. This might mean saying "no" to additional responsibilities that overextend us or limiting our exposure to sources of stress. Protecting our peace means respecting our own needs and prioritizing our well-being, creating an inner sanctuary that remains steady despite external demands.

Self-compassion is also vital to inner peace. When we encounter obstacles or challenging emotions, rather than reacting harshly, we can respond with gentleness, acknowledging our struggles without letting them control us. Accepting our thoughts, feelings, and circumstances as they are reduces inner conflict and allows us to approach life from a centered, peaceful place.

Cultivating inner peace is an ongoing journey, a daily practice of choosing calm over chaos. It reminds us that while we may not control what happens around us, we can always find a steady, quiet place within. Inner peace becomes the compass that guides us through life, empowering us to face challenges with patience and strength.

WEEK 33

Wednesday Reflection

How have you created moments of inner peace this week?

Reflect on a practice or thought that brought you calm and centeredness.

WEEK 33

Friday Reflection

What challenges did you face that tested your sense of peace?

Consider how you responded and what you can learn from that experience.

"Forgiveness is the gift you give yourself—release the weight of yesterday to embrace the freedom of today."

THE POWER OF FORGIVENESS:
LETTING GO TO MOVE FORWARD

WEEK 34

Forgiveness is a transformative act of self-love, a choice to release ourselves from the heavy burden of past hurt and resentment. Forgiving others—and ourselves—isn't about excusing what happened; it's about letting go of the pain and reclaiming our freedom. True forgiveness requires compassion, empathy, and sometimes the willingness to understand both the other person's perspective and our own emotional reactions.

When we choose forgiveness, we reclaim our power, refusing to let past wounds dictate our present or future. Holding onto anger or resentment can feel justifiable, but it often causes more harm, as we continuously relive the hurt. By choosing forgiveness, we break free from this cycle, creating space for healing and inner peace. Forgiveness invites us to release judgments and abandon expectations that others might never meet, allowing us to move forward with clarity.

Self-forgiveness is equally vital. We all make mistakes, and learning to acknowledge our imperfections with compassion enables us to grow, rather than remain trapped in regret. Practicing self-forgiveness involves embracing our humanity, taking responsibility when necessary, and moving forward with newfound understanding and resolve.

Forgiveness is about freeing our hearts and minds, letting go of the past so we can fully embrace the present and future. By choosing forgiveness, we invite peace, healing, and personal growth, creating a foundation for a more joyful and fulfilling life.

WEEK 34

Wednesday Reflection

What or whom have you chosen to forgive this week?

Reflect on how releasing resentment has lightened your heart.

WEEK 34

Friday Reflection

How has forgiveness helped you embrace a positive outlook this week?

Consider a moment where letting go opened up space for peace or growth.

"Patience is faith in life's rhythm—trust that what's meant for you will unfold in time."

EMBRACING PATIENCE:
TRUSTING LIFE'S TIMING

WEEK 35

Patience is an act of faith—a trust that life will unfold as it's meant to, in its own perfect time. Embracing patience invites us to let go of the need for immediate results and to find joy in each stage of the journey. Often, our desire for control leads us to feel frustrated when things don't progress as quickly as we'd like. Yet, by practicing patience, we cultivate acceptance, allowing life's natural rhythm to reveal itself in ways that serve our growth and well-being.

Patience teaches us that every moment, even the quiet or challenging ones, has something valuable to offer. When we learn to wait with grace, we uncover growth and wisdom in these in-between moments. Whether we're working toward a career goal, pursuing a personal aspiration, or navigating a relationship, the journey itself holds essential lessons. Embracing patience enables us to engage fully with life, recognizing that setbacks and delays are often necessary parts of the process.

To practice patience, it helps to shift our perspective. Rather than fixating on what hasn't happened yet, we can choose to appreciate what's happening right now. This outlook not only soothes frustration but also fosters gratitude for the present moment. By trusting life's timing, we free ourselves from the constant anxiety of trying to "get somewhere" and instead savor each step along the way.

Patience is a gift we give to ourselves. It allows us to live with greater ease, finding contentment and faith in the journey rather than waiting solely for a specific outcome. In choosing patience, we create a life filled with calm, trust, and resilience.

WEEK 35

Wednesday Reflection

How have you practiced patience this week?

Reflect on a situation where waiting allowed you to grow or learn something valuable.

WEEK 35

Friday Reflection

What have you gained from trusting life's timing this week?

Consider how practicing patience has influenced your outlook or relationships.

> "Resilience is not about avoiding challenges but learning to grow through them with strength."

BUILDING MENTAL RESILIENCE:
BOUNCING BACK FROM SETBACKS

WEEK 36

Mental resilience is the inner strength that allows us to face life's challenges with courage and perseverance. Building resilience is about developing a mindset that empowers us to overcome setbacks, adapt to change, and stay focused on growth, no matter what we encounter. With resilience, each obstacle becomes an opportunity to strengthen our resolve and learn more about ourselves.

To cultivate resilience, we must embrace our capacity for growth and change. When difficulties arise, rather than asking, "Why is this happening?" we can ask, "What can I learn from this?" This shift in perspective helps us view challenges as stepping stones rather than barriers. Resilience also involves self-compassion; instead of being hard on ourselves when things don't go as planned, we acknowledge our efforts and choose to move forward with grace.

Resilience is often built through small, everyday practices—setting goals, managing stress, and maintaining a positive outlook. Each small act of perseverance strengthens our ability to face bigger challenges. Additionally, connecting with supportive people helps us feel grounded and less isolated, reminding us that we don't have to face challenges alone.

Resilience is about choosing hope and strength over defeat. It's the commitment to keep moving forward, knowing that with each setback, we gain insight, endurance, and courage.

WEEK 36

Wednesday Reflection

How have you demonstrated resilience this week?

Reflect on a challenge you faced and how you stayed focused on growth.

WEEK 36

Friday Reflection

What have you learned from your setbacks this week?

Consider how resilience has helped you find a positive way forward.

> "Kindness transforms; every small act creates ripples of connection and healing."

PRACTICING KINDNESS:
SMALL ACTS WITH A BIG IMPACT

WEEK 37

Kindness is a transformative force that touches lives deeply—benefiting both those who give and those who receive it. Practicing kindness means choosing to approach others with compassion, empathy, and respect, even when it may not be the easiest path. Each act of kindness, no matter how small, has a powerful ripple effect, creating waves of positivity that uplift everyone involved. The practice of kindness reminds us of our shared humanity and builds bridges of connection.

Kindness doesn't have to be grand or elaborate; it's often the smallest gestures that make the greatest impact. A warm smile to a stranger, a listening ear for a friend in need, or a sincere "thank you" to someone who feels overlooked can brighten someone's day and remind them that they are valued. Acts of kindness, especially those given without expectation of anything in return, demonstrate a genuine care and connection that leaves a lasting impact.

Engaging in kindness is also beneficial for our own well-being. Studies show that kind acts can increase feelings of happiness, reduce stress, and even improve physical health. By focusing on giving without expectation, we cultivate a mindset of abundance, reinforcing the belief that we have something meaningful to offer the world. This approach to life nourishes our sense of purpose and deepens our connections with others.

Kindness is an invitation to bring light into the world. It's a choice to make each interaction a little gentler, each word a little kinder, each moment of support a little more sincere. By practicing kindness in this way, we contribute to a more compassionate world, one small act at a time. In choosing kindness daily, we build a legacy of empathy, warmth, and love.

WEEK 37

Wednesday Reflection

What acts of kindness have you practiced this week?

Reflect on a moment where you brought joy or support to someone else.

WEEK 37

Friday Reflection

How has kindness impacted your outlook this week?

Consider how showing compassion has influenced your perspective on relationships or life.

"What you've been chasing out there has been whispering within you all along. Trust the hush of your knowing. Let it lead you—not with bravado, but with brave tenderness."

EMBRACING VULNERABILITY:
FINDING STRENGTH IN OPENNESS

WEEK 38

Vulnerability is often misunderstood as a weakness, but in reality, it is one of the greatest sources of strength and courage we can cultivate. Embracing vulnerability means allowing ourselves to be open to the possibility of discomfort or hurt, while still choosing to share our true thoughts, feelings, and experiences with others. When we allow ourselves to be vulnerable, we don't just deepen our connections with others; we also strengthen our resilience and cultivate courage within ourselves.

Being vulnerable invites us to let down our guard, shedding the need to appear flawless or in control. It's about trusting that by revealing our authentic selves, we lay a foundation for genuine connection and understanding. Vulnerability builds bridges in relationships—whether with friends, family members, or colleagues. When we show others who we truly are, we give them permission to do the same, creating spaces where people feel valued and seen. By sharing our struggles, fears, and dreams openly, we foster relationships built on mutual respect and empathy, not just surface-level interactions.

This openness can feel intimidating, especially if we've experienced rejection or hurt in the past. But with each act of vulnerability, we build confidence in our ability to navigate life's emotional landscape. Vulnerability doesn't mean sharing everything with everyone; rather, it's about choosing to be authentic with those who have shown they can hold space for our truths. In doing so, we cultivate self-acceptance, allowing us to live as our genuine selves.

Embracing vulnerability is an act of bravery. It empowers us to live openly and form deeper connections, knowing that fulfillment and true connection come from living a life of honesty and authenticity.

WEEK 38

Wednesday Reflection

How have you embraced vulnerability this week?

Reflect on a moment where you shared openly with someone and how it deepened your connection.

WEEK 38

Friday Reflection

What has vulnerability taught you about yourself this week?

Consider how openness has helped you find strength or clarity.

> "Your body is a living prayer, a quiet revolution of breath and bone. Shift your gaze and the world changes shape—what once felt heavy begins to sing."

PRACTICING GRATITUDE FOR YOUR BODY:
EMBRACING PHYSICAL WELL-BEING

WEEK 39

Our bodies are extraordinary vessels that support us in every step of our lives, yet it's easy to overlook the invaluable role they play. Practicing gratitude for our bodies means acknowledging their strength, resilience, and the countless ways they enable us to experience life. It's a shift in focus from appearance to appreciation, a recognition of all that our bodies do for us each day, allowing us to live, connect, and grow.

This practice begins with mindfulness. Taking moments to tune into our bodies—feeling sensations, breathing deeply, and noticing our physical capabilities—is a way of honoring ourselves. Whether it's the ability to walk, run, stretch, or simply sit in stillness, our bodies deserve acknowledgment for everything they allow us to experience. Practicing gratitude also means treating our bodies with kindness—providing nourishment, rest, and movement that supports and revitalizes us.

Embracing gratitude for our bodies requires self-compassion. It's easy to fixate on perceived imperfections or limitations, but by shifting our perspective, we learn to appreciate all that our bodies accomplish each day. This practice not only enhances our physical well-being but also positively influences our self-image, helping us cultivate a sense of confidence and pride in who we are. By acknowledging our body's value, we encourage ourselves to live more fully, with a sense of freedom and joy in the present.

Practicing gratitude for our bodies is an act of self-love. It's a way of saying "thank you" to ourselves and acknowledging that our bodies are our lifelong companions, deserving of respect, care, and deep appreciation. Through this practice, we create a foundation of well-being that strengthens both our physical and emotional health.

WEEK 39

Wednesday Reflection

How have you expressed gratitude for your body this week?

Reflect on a moment where you honored or nurtured your physical well-being.

WEEK 39

Friday Reflection

In what ways has caring for your body influenced your self-esteem this week?

Consider how gratitude for your physical self has impacted your overall well-being.

"Stillness is not the absence of movement—it is the presence of meaning. Sit beside yourself long enough, and you will hear the ancient echo of your own becoming."

EMBRACING SOLITUDE:
FINDING COMFORT IN YOUR OWN COMPANY

WEEK 40

Solitude is often mistaken for loneliness, but in truth, it can be a profound source of comfort, clarity, and self-connection. Embracing solitude means learning to enjoy our own company, finding peace in moments of quiet, and using this time to reflect, recharge, and grow. Solitude allows us to connect with our inner selves, free from distractions and external influences, giving us the space to understand and appreciate who we are at our core.

Spending time alone deepens our self-awareness, providing us the freedom to think, feel, and explore without the weight of others' expectations. In solitude, we have the opportunity to reflect on our goals, dreams, and values, aligning our actions with what truly matters to us. This time alone also nurtures creativity and introspection, opening doors to new insights, ideas, and a more profound understanding of ourselves.

Embracing solitude isn't about isolating ourselves from others; rather, it's about carving out intentional moments for self-reflection and renewal. These quiet times help us build a strong relationship with our inner self, fostering a sense of wholeness and self-reliance. When we feel comfortable and at peace in our own company, we approach relationships and life with a greater sense of balance, knowing we are complete on our own.

Solitude is a gift, a time to reconnect with our inner world and to nurture our own well-being. By embracing these moments of aloneness, we cultivate a sense of peace that enriches all areas of our lives, enabling us to navigate the world with clarity, calm, and confidence.

WEEK 40

Wednesday Reflection

How have you embraced solitude this week?

Reflect on a moment where spending time alone brought you clarity or peace.

WEEK 40

Friday Reflection

What have you discovered about yourself in moments of solitude this week?

Consider how connecting with your inner self has influenced your perspective or choices.

"Fear only guards the door to what you most deeply desire. Walk through, not because you're unafraid, but because what's waiting inside you is too sacred to leave behind."

CULTIVATING CREATIVITY:
TAPPING INTO YOUR INNER ARTIST

WEEK 41

Creativity is an inherent part of who we are—a vibrant expression of our unique experiences, emotions, and perspectives. Cultivating creativity means allowing ourselves the freedom to explore, experiment, and create without judgment. By tapping into our creative side, we connect with our inner artist, discover hidden parts of ourselves, and experience the joy of bringing something new into the world.

Creativity extends beyond traditional art forms; it can be found in cooking, writing, problem-solving, or even in how we approach our daily routines. Each of us has a personal style of creativity waiting to be explored. By giving ourselves permission to create, we invite playfulness, curiosity, and openness into our lives. These qualities not only enhance our creative endeavors but also foster personal growth and bring renewed energy to our daily experiences.

Nurturing creativity also builds resilience. Not everything we create will turn out as envisioned, and embracing this truth teaches us patience and flexibility. The creative process is a journey of experimenting, learning, and trying again, which builds confidence in our ability to adapt and persevere. Through creativity, we start to see the world with fresh eyes, finding inspiration in the ordinary and delight in the act of self-expression.

Creativity is ultimately a celebration of our inner selves. It's about embracing our unique voice and bringing our ideas to life without fear. By nurturing our creativity, we deepen our connection with ourselves and experience life with a sense of wonder, excitement, and fulfillment.

WEEK 41

Wednesday Reflection

How have you tapped into your creativity this week?

Reflect on an activity or expression that allowed you to explore your creative side.

WEEK 41

Friday Reflection

What have you learned about yourself through creativity this week?

Consider how expressing yourself artistically has influenced your mood or perspective.

> "The heart unclutters when we stop gripping what's already gone. Let go. Let light in. Make space for what breathes life into you."

EMBRACING SIMPLICITY:
FINDING JOY IN LESS

WEEK 42

In a world that often equates "more" with success, choosing simplicity is a radical act of self-care. Embracing simplicity means focusing on what truly matters, letting go of excess, and finding joy in life's small, meaningful moments. This practice encourages us to prioritize quality over quantity, creating space for inner peace, clarity, and fulfillment. Simplicity offers a pathway to reconnect with what genuinely enriches our lives, free from the noise of unnecessary distractions.

Choosing simplicity invites us to evaluate what brings us real happiness and what merely adds clutter—both in our surroundings and in our minds. By releasing unnecessary possessions, commitments, and habits, we create space to fully appreciate and enjoy what we have. Embracing simplicity can mean decluttering our living spaces, streamlining our routines, or learning to say "no" to things that drain our energy. This intentional approach helps us reclaim our time and focus, allowing us to engage more deeply with people and activities that bring us joy.

Living simply also cultivates gratitude. When we focus on life's essentials, we appreciate each moment more fully, savoring the beauty of nature, meaningful conversations, and moments of rest. Simplicity encourages us to live mindfully, recognizing that true wealth lies in experiences, connections, and inner peace rather than in material accumulation.

Embracing simplicity is about aligning our lives with our values. It's a choice to live intentionally, to find joy in having less, and to find fulfillment in what truly matters. By living simply, we create a life that feels authentic, balanced, and deeply satisfying—a life where every moment holds meaning.

WEEK 42

Wednesday Reflection

How have you embraced simplicity this week?

Reflect on a moment where you chose to focus on the essentials and how it brought you peace.

WEEK 42

Friday Reflection

What have you gained from living more simply this week?

Consider how embracing minimalism has influenced your sense of contentment and clarity.

> "You were never meant to outrun your soul. Slow down. Listen for the rhythm that nourishes you, not just the one that earns applause."

PRACTICING SELF-COMPASSION:
BEING KIND TO YOURSELF

WEEK 43

Self-compassion is the practice of treating ourselves with the same kindness, understanding, and patience that we would offer to a close friend. It's about showing gentleness toward ourselves, especially when things don't go as planned or when we feel disappointed. Practicing self-compassion allows us to release self-criticism and embrace the reality that mistakes and setbacks are simply part of the growth process.

At its core, self-compassion is about recognizing our humanity. We are all imperfect, and we will inevitably make mistakes, encounter challenges, and fall short of our own expectations at times. However, rather than judging ourselves harshly, we can choose to respond with empathy and understanding. Self-compassion reminds us that we are deserving of love and acceptance, even when we feel we're not at our best. This attitude helps us build resilience, as it teaches us to approach ourselves with forgiveness and patience.

To cultivate self-compassion, we can start by being mindful of our inner dialogue. Replacing self-critical thoughts with supportive, affirming ones can help us create a kinder relationship with ourselves. Self-compassion also involves letting go of past mistakes, accepting that we did our best at the time, and choosing to move forward without lingering guilt. Embracing this mindset not only boosts self-esteem but also reduces stress, making us more resilient and capable of facing life's challenges with grace.

Self-compassion is a gift we give to ourselves—a practice that fosters inner peace, self-acceptance, and emotional resilience. When we approach life with kindness and understanding, we open our hearts to a greater sense of well-being and fulfillment.

WEEK 43

Wednesday Reflection

How have you practiced self-compassion this week?

Reflect on a moment where you chose kindness over self-criticism and how it affected your well-being.

WEEK 43

Friday Reflection

In what ways has self-compassion influenced your outlook this week?

Consider how being gentle with yourself has impacted your resilience or self-esteem.

"Not every open door is yours to walk through. Some things bloom only when you learn the holy art of saying no."

BUILDING HEALTHY BOUNDARIES:
HONORING YOUR NEEDS AND LIMITS

WEEK 44

Healthy boundaries are essential for maintaining balance, preserving our energy, and respecting our needs. Building boundaries involves understanding our personal limits and communicating them to others in a way that fosters mutual respect. Boundaries are not barriers; they are tools that allow us to prioritize our well-being and create a foundation for showing up fully in our relationships, without feeling overwhelmed or depleted.

Creating healthy boundaries starts with self-awareness. By identifying what feels comfortable and sustainable, we gain clarity on when our limits are being tested or crossed. Boundaries can take various forms, from setting limits on our time and energy to expressing our emotional needs. Saying "no" when necessary is an act of self-respect, not selfishness. It allows us to focus on what truly matters, preventing burnout and keeping our energy aligned with our values and goals.

Setting boundaries can be challenging, especially if we're accustomed to prioritizing others' needs over our own. However, establishing boundaries doesn't mean we're shutting people out; rather, it means showing up in relationships in a way that honors both our needs and the needs of others. Practicing clear and compassionate communication is key, as it helps create boundaries that support healthy, balanced relationships, where everyone's needs are acknowledged and valued.

Building boundaries is a powerful act of self-love. It's about giving ourselves permission to protect our well-being and honoring the importance of self-care. Healthy boundaries create a foundation for strong, respectful connections—with ourselves and others—and allow us to live with authenticity and integrity.

WEEK 44

Wednesday Reflection

How have you practiced setting boundaries this week?

Reflect on a situation where you honored your needs and how it impacted your well-being.

WEEK 44

Friday Reflection

What have you learned about yourself through boundary-setting this week?

Consider how respecting your limits has influenced your energy and relationships.

> "Every fall is a rehearsal for your rising. You are not the stumble—you are the steady breath that stands back up."

CULTIVATING OPTIMISM:
SEEING THE GOOD IN EVERY SITUATION

WEEK 45

Optimism is a mindset that encourages us to focus on the positive, even when circumstances are challenging. It's not about ignoring difficulties or pretending everything is perfect; it's about choosing to see opportunities for growth and solutions rather than dwelling solely on problems. Cultivating optimism allows us to approach life with hope, resilience, and a sense of possibility, helping us navigate both the highs and lows with grace.

An optimistic outlook often begins with gratitude—appreciating the small joys and blessings that each day brings. By focusing on what we're thankful for, we shift our perspective away from what's lacking and toward what's abundant. Optimism also involves reframing challenges and setbacks as opportunities for learning. Each difficult moment can teach us something valuable, whether it's patience, strength, adaptability, or problem-solving skills. By viewing obstacles as stepping stones rather than roadblocks, we empower ourselves to keep moving forward.

Choosing optimism doesn't mean we'll never feel discouraged or struggle through tough times. Rather, it reminds us that after every setback, there's the potential for a new beginning. When we consciously choose to see the good, we strengthen our mental resilience, making it easier to handle life's ups and downs with courage and grace. Additionally, optimism often inspires those around us, creating a ripple effect of positivity and hope that uplifts others as well.

Optimism is a choice—a way of approaching life that empowers us to embrace both the beauty and challenges of our journey. By cultivating this mindset, we open ourselves to joy, growth, and the possibility of a brighter future, even when the path forward isn't immediately clear.

WEEK 45

Wednesday Reflection

How have you practiced optimism this week?

Reflect on a moment where you chose to see the good in a situation and how it affected your mood.

WEEK 45

Friday Reflection

In what ways has optimism influenced your outlook this week?

Consider how focusing on possibilities has impacted your approach to challenges or relationships.

> "Perfection is a myth that steals your joy. What is real is your becoming—flawed, sacred, and brilliantly unfinished."

BUILDING SELF-DISCIPLINE:
CREATING HABITS THAT SUPPORT YOUR GOALS

WEEK 46

Self-discipline is the foundation of consistent progress, allowing us to honor our commitments even when initial motivation wanes. It's the skill that helps us create habits aligned with our goals, guiding us steadily toward the life we envision. Building self-discipline is a journey of patience, practice, and persistence, as each step reinforces our ability to stay on track.

The journey to self-discipline begins with clarity—understanding exactly what we want to achieve and, more importantly, why it matters to us. When our goals are meaningful and resonate with our values, we're more likely to stay committed through challenges. Self-discipline also thrives within a supportive structure. This might mean setting realistic goals, planning our days, and establishing routines that foster consistency. Starting small, then gradually building on each success, creates momentum that keeps us engaged and motivated.

Self-discipline doesn't mean being rigid or overly critical of ourselves; it's about balancing commitment with self-compassion. When we experience setbacks or miss a step, self-discipline reminds us to learn from the experience rather than give up. Each time we choose to realign with our goals after a slip, we build resilience and a deeper focus on the bigger picture. This gentle yet firm approach allows us to stay dedicated while also respecting our humanity.

Self-discipline is ultimately a tool for self-empowerment. It allows us to create a life that truly reflects our values and aspirations, bringing our dreams within reach through sustained action. By cultivating self-discipline, we take control of our growth, forming habits that strengthen our journey and bring us closer to the life we want to lead.

WEEK 46

Wednesday Reflection

What steps have you taken toward your goals this week?

Reflect on a small act of self-discipline and how it contributed to your progress.

WEEK 46

Friday Reflection

In what ways has self-discipline influenced your week?

Consider how committing to your goals has impacted your sense of accomplishment or motivation.

> "Peace is not the absence of chaos, but the willingness to stay. Stay soft. Stay open. Stay here, where life is always unfolding."

PRACTICING MINDFULNESS:
BEING PRESENT IN EACH MOMENT

WEEK 47

Mindfulness is the practice of being fully present, aware of our thoughts, emotions, and surroundings without judgment. By practicing mindfulness, we connect with each moment as it unfolds, fostering a sense of calm, clarity, and gratitude for the richness of life. When we're mindful, we engage with a deeper awareness, savoring each interaction, sensation, and experience as it comes.

Mindfulness often begins with something as simple as paying attention to our breath. This grounding practice helps center us in the present, allowing us to observe our thoughts and emotions without getting swept away by them. Mindfulness teaches us to watch our inner experiences like passing clouds, understanding them without attachment. By focusing on the present moment, we naturally reduce stress, as we're not consumed by regrets about the past or anxieties about the future. This calm attentiveness builds resilience, helping us respond thoughtfully to whatever life brings.

The benefits of mindfulness extend into our relationships as well. When we listen mindfully, without distraction, we connect with others more meaningfully, creating an atmosphere of empathy and understanding. This presence enhances our relationships, allowing us to share in each other's experiences more fully. Additionally, mindfulness helps us notice and appreciate life's small, everyday joys—like the warmth of sunlight, the taste of a favorite meal, or the sound of laughter.

Mindfulness is a way of living that brings us closer to ourselves and to the world around us. By embracing each moment with openness, we cultivate peace and gratitude, enriching every aspect of our lives and helping us live with a fuller, more compassionate awareness.

WEEK 47

Wednesday Reflection

How have you practiced mindfulness this week?

Reflect on a moment where you were fully present and how it affected your experience.

WEEK 47

Friday Reflection

What has mindfulness taught you about yourself or life this week?

Consider how staying present has influenced your mood or perspective.

"Gratitude is the alchemy of enough. When you tend to the small, it grows roots that anchor you in abundance."

PRACTICING HUMILITY:
EMBRACING GROWTH OVER EGO

WEEK 48

Humility is the practice of recognizing that life is a continuous journey of learning and self-discovery. Embracing humility means acknowledging that we don't have all the answers and that our understanding is always evolving. By approaching life with curiosity and openness, we create space to grow and learn from others and from every experience we encounter. Humility doesn't require us to undervalue ourselves; instead, it invites us to see ourselves as a valuable part of something larger. It's about honoring both our own worth and the knowledge and perspectives that others bring.

Practicing humility frees us from the need to always be "right" or to have every answer. It allows us to adopt a mindset that prioritizes growth over ego, helping us see both our strengths and our areas for improvement with honesty and clarity. When we accept that we're human and capable of mistakes, we become more resilient and adaptable. This openness helps us move forward without being limited by fear of failure or judgment, knowing that every experience, even our mistakes, serves as an opportunity for learning.

Humility also deepens our relationships by encouraging us to listen, appreciate, and value others' perspectives. When we approach others with humility, we foster a sense of mutual respect and empathy, making space for genuine connections and rich, insightful exchanges. This openness not only strengthens our bonds but also broadens our understanding of the world around us, allowing us to grow beyond our own limited viewpoints.

At its core, humility is a powerful tool for personal development. By setting aside our ego and embracing lifelong learning, we cultivate a mindset that values understanding over pride. Humility invites us to be both students and teachers, enriching our lives and allowing us to embrace each new experience with an open, compassionate heart.

WEEK 48

Wednesday Reflection

How have you practiced humility this week?

Reflect on a moment where you let go of the need to be right or sought out learning over ego.

WEEK 48

Friday Reflection

In what ways has humility influenced your growth this week?

Consider how embracing a learning mindset has impacted your interactions or perspective.

> "Life isn't a puzzle to be solved, but a path to be shaped—one choice, one breath, one act of courage at a time."

FOSTERING SELF-BELIEF:
TRUSTING IN YOUR UNIQUE PATH

WEEK 49

Self-belief is the foundation upon which all our pursuits rest—a quiet, yet powerful confidence in our abilities, resilience, and sense of purpose. Fostering self-belief means trusting in our unique path, even when it feels uncertain or filled with challenges. It's about having faith that we possess what we need to achieve our goals, and knowing that we are worthy of success and fulfillment.

Self-belief begins by recognizing and appreciating our strengths, acknowledging our passions, and celebrating each accomplishment, whether big or small. This confidence isn't based on external validation; rather, it's anchored in a deep inner assurance that we are capable and deserving. When we foster self-belief, we give ourselves the freedom to dream boldly, take risks, and grow through each experience, whether we succeed immediately or learn from setbacks.

Challenges are inevitable, but self-belief gives us the strength to persevere. It reminds us that setbacks are not failures, but part of the learning process, helping us refine our path. Each step forward, no matter how small, contributes to our growth, building resilience and focus. Self-belief empowers us to pursue our dreams with conviction and to approach each endeavor with the knowledge that we are on our own journey—a journey we are fully equipped to navigate.

Fostering self-belief is about trusting our unique path and embracing the gifts and talents that define us. It's a commitment to growth and a recognition of our potential. By cultivating self-belief, we build a life that mirrors our true potential, one where we honor our individual journey with confidence and purpose.

WEEK 49

Wednesday Reflection

How have you fostered self-belief this week?

Reflect on a moment where you trusted in your abilities or celebrated a personal strength.

WEEK 49

Friday Reflection

In what ways has self-belief influenced your actions this week?

Consider how trusting yourself has impacted your confidence and decision-making.

"You are not starting over; you are beginning again, wiser now, stitched with the grace of every moment that didn't break you."

PRACTICING ACCEPTANCE:
EMBRACING LIFE AS IT IS

WEEK 50

Acceptance is a powerful practice that encourages us to approach life as it unfolds, without resistance or wishing for things to be different. Practicing acceptance doesn't mean we stop pursuing change or growth; rather, it means finding peace in the present, even when circumstances aren't ideal. By accepting ourselves, our experiences, and others as they are, we release frustration and invite inner peace and balance.

Acceptance begins with self-compassion. When we embrace our imperfections, we stop battling against our own limitations and start viewing ourselves with kindness and understanding. Extending this practice to our relationships allows us to let go of the urge to control others, fostering an environment where we appreciate each person as they are. This sense of acceptance nurtures empathy, building deeper and more meaningful connections.

Living with acceptance teaches us to be fully present, appreciating each moment without attaching ourselves to specific outcomes. While it's healthy to set goals and strive toward our aspirations, acceptance reminds us that we are already whole and complete as we are. This perspective helps alleviate stress and anxiety by allowing us to let go of the "shoulds" and embrace reality just as it is.

Acceptance is about cultivating a life filled with peace and contentment. By releasing resistance, we nurture a mindset that honors life's beauty and complexities, enabling us to approach each day with greater joy, resilience, and gratitude.

WEEK 50

Wednesday Reflection

How have you practiced acceptance this week?

Reflect on a moment where you let go of control or embraced a situation as it was.

WEEK 50

Friday Reflection

In what ways has acceptance influenced your well-being this week?

Consider how letting go of resistance has impacted your mood or outlook.

"Look back with mercy, look within with honesty. It is in the quiet excavation of your story that your next chapter begins."

CULTIVATING CURIOSITY:
EMBRACING LIFE'S WONDERS

WEEK 51

Curiosity is a mindset that invites us to explore life with an open heart, a desire to learn, and a sense of wonder. When we cultivate curiosity, we commit to seeing the world in a fresh, inquisitive way, embracing each experience, idea, and interaction as an opportunity to expand our understanding. Curiosity keeps us from becoming complacent, reminding us that there is always more to discover about ourselves, others, and the world around us.

Practicing curiosity encourages us to step out of our comfort zones and try new things. When we approach challenges with a curious mindset, we are less likely to be hindered by fear of failure. Instead, we become willing to take risks, viewing each experience as a chance to grow, whether or not it leads to immediate success. Curiosity fosters resilience, allowing us to transform setbacks into stepping stones for further exploration.

Curiosity also strengthens our relationships. When we listen to others with genuine interest, we learn to appreciate their unique perspectives and experiences. This openness fosters empathy, allowing us to build meaningful connections across different walks of life. By approaching conversations with curiosity, we not only deepen our relationships but also enrich our own understanding of the world.

Ultimately, cultivating curiosity adds depth and excitement to our lives. It fuels a lifelong love of learning and reminds us that every day brings new opportunities for discovery. By embracing curiosity, we unlock the beauty of life's mysteries, finding joy in both the known and unknown aspects of our journey.

WEEK 51

Wednesday Reflection

How have you cultivated curiosity this week?

Reflect on a moment when you approached a situation or person with openness and wonder.

WEEK 51

Friday Reflection

What has curiosity taught you about yourself or life this week?

Consider how embracing new experiences has influenced your perspective.

> "You are not who you were—and that is something to honor. Let joy rise in the in-between, in the miracle of your unfolding."

EMBRACING JOY:
FINDING HAPPINESS IN SMALL MOMENTS

WEEK 52

Joy is a conscious choice, a practice of seeing the world with appreciation and delight for the small moments that make up our daily lives. Embracing joy means choosing to find happiness in the ordinary: the warmth of sunlight on our skin, a comforting meal, laughter shared with friends, or the satisfaction of a task completed. By embracing these small, often simple experiences, we realize that happiness is woven into the fabric of everyday life, always available if we open ourselves to it.

Cultivating joy starts with mindfulness, the practice of being fully present and noticing what's happening around us. When we pause to pay attention, we become more attuned to the richness of life, seeing beauty in places we might otherwise overlook. By staying present, we learn to focus on what's abundant rather than on what's lacking, creating a sense of gratitude and fulfillment. This shift in focus invites happiness into each day, transforming even ordinary moments into sources of joy.

Embracing joy also requires letting go of perfectionism. Life doesn't need to be flawless to be fulfilling. Instead, joy often comes from accepting things as they are and celebrating the beauty of imperfection. When we release the need for control or ideal outcomes, we open ourselves to unexpected happiness, even in difficult times. This acceptance builds resilience, allowing us to approach life with optimism and flexibility.

Joy is an act of gratitude and celebration, a reminder that each moment is precious. By cultivating joy, we learn to experience life more fully, building a foundation of positivity and contentment that influences every aspect of our well-being. Through this practice, we create a life that is rich with meaning, filled with appreciation for the small but powerful moments that bring us happiness.

WEEK 52

Wednesday Reflection

How have you embraced joy this week?

Reflect on a small moment that brought you happiness and how it impacted your day.

WEEK 52

Friday Reflection

In what ways has finding joy influenced your outlook this week?

Consider how appreciating the small things has enhanced your well-being.

www.ingramcontent.com/pod-product-compliance
Lightning Source LLC
Chambersburg PA
CBHW070320010526
44107CB00004B/372